Multiplication
MASTER

Lisa Arias

rourkeeducationalmedia.com

Before Reading:

Building Academic Vocabulary and Background Knowledge

Before reading a book, it is important to tap into what your child or students already know about the topic. This will help them develop their vocabulary, increase their reading comprehension, and make connections across the curriculum.

1. Look at the cover of the book. What will this book be about?
2. What do you already know about the topic?
3. Let's study the Table of Contents. What will you learn about in the book's chapters?
4. What would you like to learn about this topic? Do you think you might learn about it from this book? Why or why not?
5. Use a reading journal to write about your knowledge of this topic. Record what you already know about the topic and what you hope to learn about the topic.
6. Read the book.
7. In your reading journal, record what you learned about the topic and your response to the book.
8. After reading the book complete the activities below.

Content Area Vocabulary
Read the list. What do these words mean?

commutative property of
    multiplication

digit

distributive property

divisibility

double

factor

multiplication

multiplication property of one

multiplication property of zero

product

sum

After Reading:

Comprehension and Extension Activity

After reading the book, work on the following questions with your child or students in order to check their level of reading comprehension and content mastery.

1. Explain why the order of the factors being multiplied does not affect the product. (Summarize)
2. Which multiplication rule is the easiest for you to remember? Which is the most difficult? (Text to self connection)
3. How are the rules for multiplying by 2 and 4 connected? (Summarize)
4. How does understanding the tricks to multiplying help you? (Text to self connection)
5. What is the multiplication trick when you multiply by 3? (Summarize)

Extension Activity

Put your multiplication rules to the test! You will need a deck of playing cards or dominoes. Test yourself by laying down two cards or dominoes and find the product using the rules you learned. Which rules are easy for you to follow? Which are difficult? Brainstorm ways you can get better at remembering the more difficult rules.

Table of Contents

Multiplication Chart 4

Simple Rules 6

Multiply by Doubling 8

Multiply by Skip Counting 10

Add a Zero 12

Distribute 14

Write It Twice 16

Add the Product's Digits 18

Rhyme Time 24

Let's Review! 26

Factor Hunt 28

Glossary 30

Index 31

Websites to Visit 31

About the Author 32

Multiplication Chart

Divisibility rules are just the right tools
to make **multiplication** facts oh, so cool!

Before we start, let's take a look at a multiplication chart.

X	0	1	2	3	4	5	6	7	8	9	10	11	12
0	0	0	0	0	0	0	0	0	0	0	0	0	0
1	0	1	2	3	4	5	6	7	8	9	10	11	12
2	0	2	4	6	8	10	12	14	16	18	20	22	24
3	0	3	6	9	12	15	18	21	24	27	30	33	36
4	0	4	8	12	16	20	24	28	32	36	40	44	48
5	0	5	10	15	20	25	30	35	40	45	50	55	60
6	0	6	12	18	24	30	36	42	48	54	60	66	72
7	0	7	14	21	28	35	42	49	56	63	70	77	84
8	0	8	16	24	32	40	48	56	64	72	80	88	96
9	0	9	18	27	36	45	54	63	72	81	90	99	108
10	0	10	20	30	40	50	60	70	80	90	100	110	120
11	0	11	22	33	44	55	66	77	88	99	110	121	132
12	0	12	24	36	48	60	72	84	96	108	120	132	144

What a relief to know that the diagonal splits the table in two. Look closely and you will see both sides are identical.

The **commutative property of multiplication** lets you switch the order of the factors without changing the **product**.

3 × 4 = 12 and **4 × 3 = 12**
Factors   Product   Factors   Product

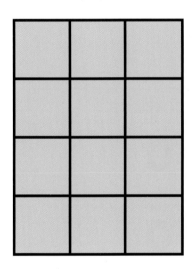 =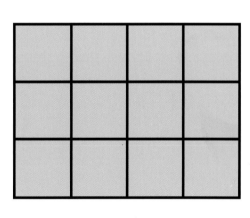

3 × 4   =   4 × 3

12   =   12

Simple Rules

Multiply by Zero and One

Let's start with zero the hero!

Any number multiplied by zero equals zero.

No matter the number, big or small, this is always true.
It is thanks to the **multiplication property of zero** rule.

Factors   Product

$$0 \times 3 = 0$$

$$2 \times 0 = 0$$

$$0 \times 0 = 0$$

$$0 \times 1,000,000 = 0$$

Time for some fun and multiply by 1!

Any **factor** multiplied by one equals that number.

This is always true, thanks to the
multiplication property of one rule.

Factors	Product
1 × 1	= 1
1 × 8	= 8
12 × 1	= 12
576 × 1	= 576

Multiply by Doubling

Multiply by 2

Multiplying by 2 is easy to do!

Just **double** the factor being multiplied by 2.

$$\text{Factors} \quad \text{Product}$$
$$2 \times 9 = 18$$
$$9 + 9$$

It's always true, all products of 2
create even numbers for me and you!

Time to play school. Which numbers are products of 2?

1 18 9 16 5 19

21

14 11 23 7 10

13

8 2 20 4 3

24 15 6 12 22

17

Multiply by 4

Now that you know your 2s, multiplying by 4 won't be a bore!

Just double the factor being multiplied by 4 not once, but twice.

$$4 \times 3 = 12$$

$$3 + 3 + 3 + 3$$

$$6 \quad + \quad 6$$

$$4 \times 5 = 20$$

$$5 + 5 + 5 + 5$$

$$10 \quad + \quad 10$$

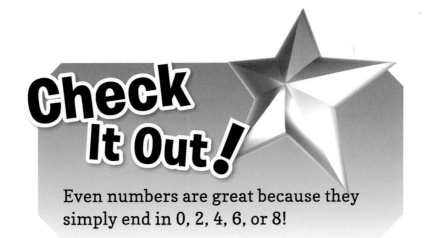

Check It Out!

Even numbers are great because they simply end in 0, 2, 4, 6, or 8!

Multiply by Skip Counting

Multiply by 5

Let's dive into multiplying by 5.

Skip counting by 5 is easy to do.
To skip count by 5, count every fifth number.
Once you get started you will discover a pattern or two.

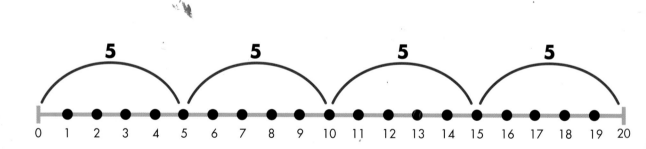

$5 \times 1 = 5$

$5 \times 7 = 35$

$5 \times 2 = 10$

$5 \times 8 = 40$

$5 \times 3 = 15$

$5 \times 9 = 45$

$5 \times 4 = 20$

$5 \times 10 = 50$

$5 \times 5 = 25$

$5 \times 11 = 55$

$5 \times 6 = 30$

$5 \times 12 = 60$

It's always true. Products of 5 end in 5 or our hero, the zero.

Multiply by 5		
Even Factors (split the factor in half and add a zero)		Odd Factors (always end in 5)
$5 \times 2 = 10$	Half of 2 is 1	$5 \times 1 = 5$
$5 \times 4 = 20$	Half of 4 is 2	$5 \times 3 = 15$
$5 \times 6 = 30$	Half of 6 is 3	$5 \times 5 = 25$
$5 \times 8 = 40$	Half of 8 is 4	$5 \times 7 = 35$
$5 \times 10 = 50$	Half of 10 is 5	$5 \times 9 = 45$
$5 \times 12 = 60$	Half of 12 is 6	$5 \times 11 = 55$

Add a Zero

Multiply by 10

Multiplying by 10 is as easy as pie.
Just add a zero to the factor. Come on. Let's give it a try.

$1 \times 10 = 10$

$2 \times 10 = 20$

$3 \times 10 = 30$

$4 \times 10 = 40$

$5 \times 10 = 50$

$6 \times 10 = 60$

$7 \times 10 = 70$

$8 \times 10 = 80$

$9 \times 10 = 90$

$10 \times 10 = 100$

$11 \times 10 = 110$

$12 \times 10 = 120$

It's always true, every product of 10 ends in zero.

I spy with my little eye the products of 10.
Can you guess the missing factors of 10?

90	70
40	110
120	30
50	80
20	100
60	10

Distribute

Multiply by 12

You will soon see, the key to multiplying by 12 is the **distributive property**!

It is really cool to split 12 up into groups of 10 and 2. Add those facts and you are through!

$$3 \times 12 = 36$$

Factors   Product

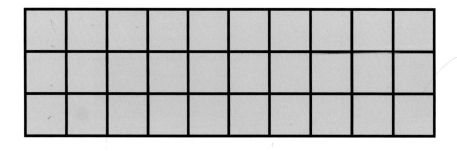 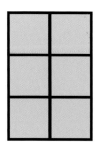

(3 × 10)   +   (3 × 2)

30   +   6

30 + 6 = 36

3 × 12

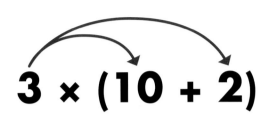

3 × (10 + 2)

30 + 6 = 36

	Think of 10s	Think of 2s	Add Products
12 × 2	10 × 2 = 20	2 × 2 = 4	20 + 4 = 24
12 × 3	10 × 3 = 30	2 × 3 = 6	30 + 6 = 36
12 × 4	10 × 4 = 40	2 × 4 = 8	40 + 8 = 48
12 × 5	10 × 5 = 50	2 × 5 = 10	50 + 10 = 60
12 × 6	10 × 6 = 60	2 × 6 = 12	60 + 12 = 72
12 × 7	10 × 7 = 70	2 × 7 = 14	70 + 14 = 84
12 × 8	10 × 8 = 80	2 × 8 = 16	80 + 16 = 96
12 × 9	10 × 9 = 90	2 × 9 = 18	90 + 18 = 108
12 × 10	10 × 10 = 100	2 × 10 = 20	100 + 20 = 120
12 × 11	10 × 11 = 110	2 × 11 = 22	110 + 22 = 132
12 × 12	10 × 12 = 120	2 × 12 = 24	120 + 24 = 144

Write It Twice

Multiply by 11

Learning the 11 facts are so quick.
Writing the factor twice is the trick.

$1 \times 11 = 11$ $6 \times 11 = 66$

$2 \times 11 = 22$ $7 \times 11 = 77$

$3 \times 11 = 33$ $8 \times 11 = 88$

$4 \times 11 = 44$ $9 \times 11 = 99$

$5 \times 11 = 55$

After 11 x 9, give a few cheers
because a new pattern appears.

The **sum** of the outer digits in the product equals the middle **digit**.

$10 \times 11 = 110$ $1 + 0 = 1$

$11 \times 11 = 121$ $1 + 1 = 2$

$12 \times 11 = 132$ $1 + 2 = 3$

Time to sneak a peek at the products of 11. How many can you find?

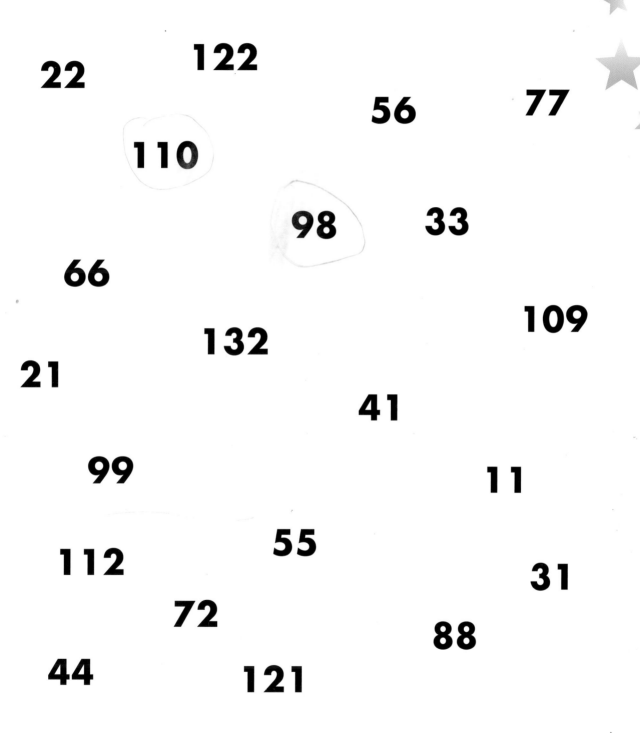

22

122

56

77

110

98

33

66

109

132

21

41

99

11

55

112

31

72

88

44

121

Add the Product's Digits

Multiply by 9

The 9s are the best ever!

Memorizing your 9s may take some time, but remember almost all of the product's digits add up to 9.

9 × 1 = 9

9 × 2 = 18

9 × 3 = 27

9 × 4 = 36

9 × 5 = 45

9 × 6 = 54

9 × 7 = 63

9 × 8 = 72

9 × 9 = 81

9 × 10 = 90

9 × 11 = 99

9 × 12 = 108

Check It Out!

1 + 8 = 9
2 + 7 = 9
3 + 6 = 9
4 + 5 = 9
9 + 0 = 9

Everything is going just fine.
Can you find the products of 9?

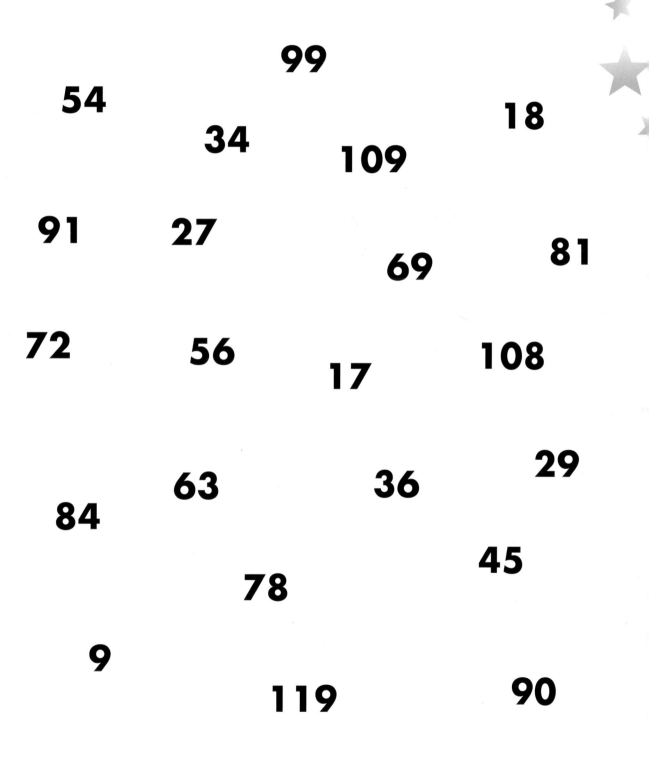

99
54
34
18
109
91 27
69
81
72 56
17
108
29
63 36
84
45
78
9
119 90

Multiply by 3

The 3s are really a breeze!

The sum of the digits of the products of 3 add up to 3, 6, or 9.

4 × 3 = 12   *1 + 2 = 3*

Factors   Product

3 × 1 = 3

3 × 2 = 6

3 × 3 = 9

3 × 4 = 12 *1 + 2 = 3*

3 × 5 = 15 *1 + 5 = 6*

3 × 6 = 18 *1 + 8 = 9*

3 × 7 = 21 *2 + 1 = 3*

3 × 8 = 24 *2 + 4 = 6*

3 × 9 = 27 *2 + 7 = 9*

3 × 10 = 30 *3 + 0 = 3*

3 × 11 = 33 *3 + 3 = 6*

3 × 12 = 36 *3 + 6 = 9*

Each product's sum is 3, 6, or 9

Take a look and see which numbers are the products of 3.

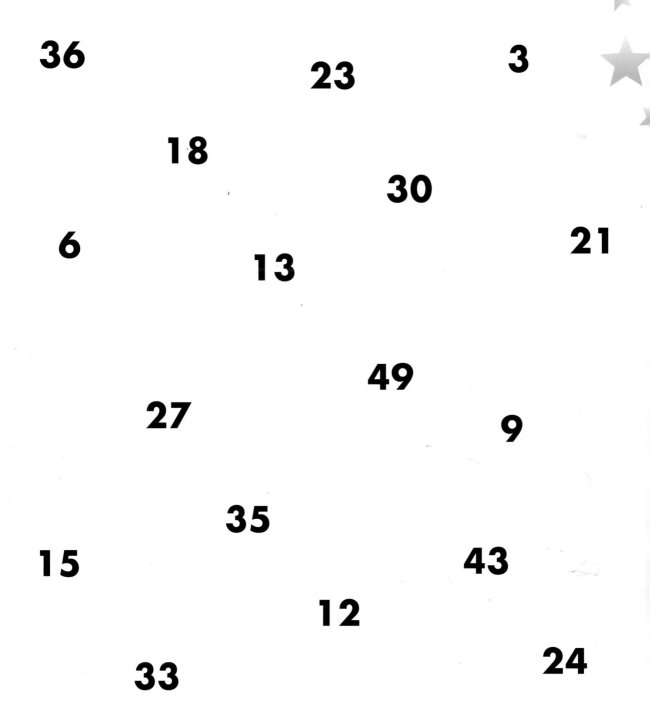

36

23

3

18

30

6

13

21

49

27

9

35

15

43

12

33

24

Multiply by 6

Let's open our bag of tricks and learn about products of 6.

The sum of the digits in the products of 6 add up to 3, 6, 9, or 12.

$6 \times 1 = 6$

$6 \times 2 = 12$ *1 + 2 = 3*

$6 \times 3 = 18$ *1 + 8 = 9*

$6 \times 4 = 24$ *2 + 4 = 6*

$6 \times 5 = 30$ *3 + 0 = 3*

$6 \times 6 = 36$ *3 + 6 = 9*

$6 \times 7 = 42$ *4 + 2 = 6*

$6 \times 8 = 48$ *4 + 8 = 12*

$6 \times 9 = 54$ *5 + 4 = 9*

$6 \times 10 = 60$ *6 + 0 = 6*

$6 \times 11 = 66$ *6 + 6 = 12*

$6 \times 12 = 72$ *7 + 2 = 9*

Each product's sum is 3, 6, 9, or 12

Take a peek to see how easy it is to relate to the products of 2, 4, 6, and 8.

Multiply 6 by 2, 4, 6, 8.	The product ends with that factor.	Fun Fact! *The first digit of the product is half of the last digit.*
6 × **2**	1**2**	Half of **2** equals 1.
6 × **4**	2**4**	Half of **4** equals 2.
6 × **6**	3**6**	Half of **6** equals 3.
6 × **8**	4**8**	Half of **8** equals 4.

Multiply by 7 and 8

It is not too late for the remaining products of 7 and 8.

Thanks to the commutative property, all the facts but a few have been taught to me and you.

X	0	1	2	3	4	5	6	7	8	9	10	11	12
0	0	0	0	0	0	0	0	0	0	0	0	0	0
1	0	1	2	3	4	5	6	7	8	9	10	11	12
2	0	2	4	6	8	10	12	14	16	18	20	22	24
3	0	3	6	9	12	15	18	21	24	27	30	33	36
4	0	4	8	12	16	20	24	28	32	36	40	44	48
5	0	5	10	15	20	25	30	35	40	45	50	55	60
6	0	6	12	18	24	30	36	42	48	54	60	66	72
7	0	7	14	21	28	35	42	49	56	63	70	77	84
8	0	8	16	24	32	40	48	56	64	72	80	88	96
9	0	9	18	27	36	45	54	63	72	81	90	99	108
10	0	10	20	30	40	50	60	70	80	90	100	110	120
11	0	11	22	33	44	55	66	77	88	99	110	121	132
12	0	12	24	36	48	60	72	84	96	108	120	132	144

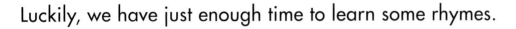

Luckily, we have just enough time to learn some rhymes.

Yes it is true,
6 times 7 is 42.

5, **6**, 7, 8!
Who do you appreciate?
56! (56 is equal to 7 x 8)

Shut the door,
8 times 8 is 64!

That is just fine,
7 times 7 is 49!

Let's Review!

Now that we have learned a thing or two, let's review!

Fun Facts up to 12 × 12

2 Double the factor

4 Double the factor twice

3 Adds up to 3, 6, or 9

6 Adds up to 3, 6, 9, or 12

9 Adds up to 9 or 18

5 Ends in 0 or 5

10 Add 0 to the factor

11 Double the factors (up to 9)

12 Add products of 10 and 2

Factor Hunt

Directions: Find the factors of the products in each picture. Check your answer with the key below.

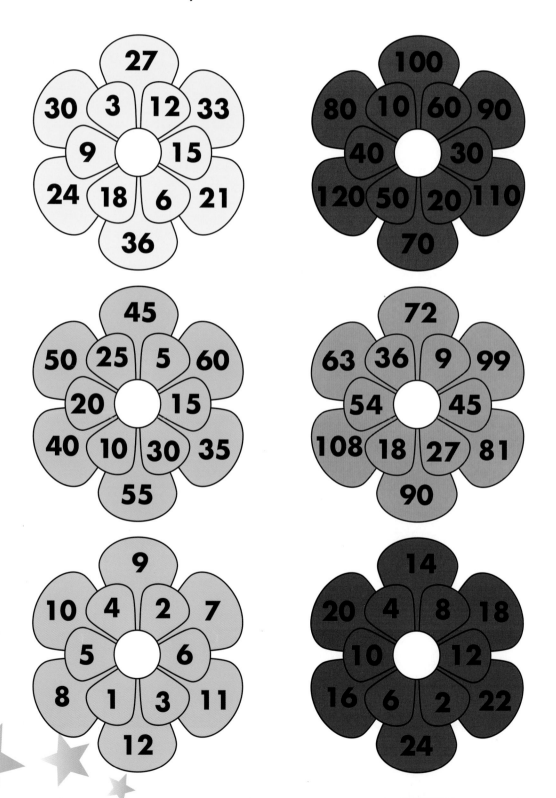

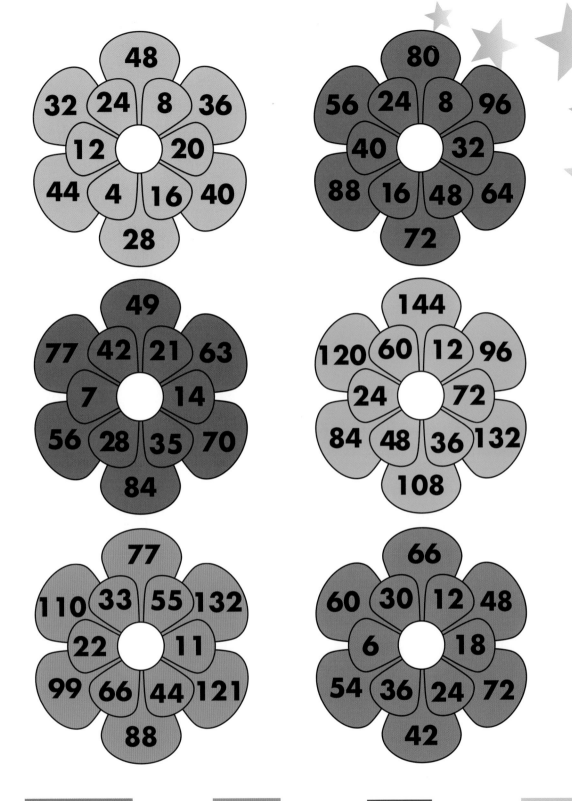

Glossary

commutative property of multiplication (kuh-MYOO-tuh-tiv PROP-ur-tee uhv muhl-tuh-pli-KEY-shuhn): if the order or the factors change, the product remains the same

digit (DIJ-it): a written symbol for any numbers 0 to 9

distributive property (dih-STRIB-yuh-tiv PROP-ur-tee): multiplying a group of numbers is equal to multiplying each number separately

divisibility (di-viz-uh-BIL-i-tee): a number that is divided evenly by another number

double (DUH-buhl): twice as much

factor (FAK-tur): the number or numbers which are multiplied together

multiplication (muhl-tuh-pli-KEY-shuhn): adding a number to itself a certain number of times

multiplication property of one (muhl-tuh-pli-KEY-shuhn PROP-ur-tee uhv wuhn): multiplying any number by one equals that number

multiplication property of zero (muhl-tuh-pli-KEY-shuhn PROP-ur-tee uhv ZEER-oh): multiplying any number by zero equals zero

product (PROD-uhkt): the answer to a multiplication problem

sum (suhm): the answer to an addition problem

Index

commutative property of multiplication 5

digit(s) 16, 18, 20, 22, 23

distributive property 14

divisibility 4

double 8, 9, 27

factor(s) 5, 6, 8, 9, 11, 12, 13, 14, 20, 27, 28

multiplication 4, 5, 6, 7

multiplication property of one 7

multiplication property of zero 6

product 5, 7, 11, 12, 13, 14, 15, 16, 17, 18, 19, 20, 21, 22, 23, 24, 28

sum 16, 20, 22

Websites to Visit

www.multiplication.com/games/all-games

www.fun4thebrain.com/mult.html

freerice.com/category

About the Author

Lisa Arias is a math teacher who lives in Tampa, Florida with her husband and two children. Her out-of-the-box thinking and teaching style guided her toward becoming an author. She enjoys playing board games and spending time with family and friends.

Meet The Author!
www.meetREMauthors.com

www.rourkeeducationalmedia.com

PHOTO CREDITS: Cover: © Franck-Boston; Page 9: © Franck-Boston; Page 20: © hidesy; Page 26: © kwaggy

Edited by: Jill Sherman

Cover and Interior design by: Tara Raymo

Library of Congress PCN Data

Multiplication Master: Divisibility Rules / Lisa Arias
(Got Math!)
 ISBN 978-1-62717-710-8 (hard cover)
 ISBN 978-1-62717-832-7 (soft cover)
 ISBN 978-1-62717-945-4 (e-Book)
Library of Congress Control Number: 2014935587

Printed in the United States of America, North Mankato, Minnesota

Also Available as: